501
Things to
pray
About

JOURNAL &
NOTEBOOK

501
Things to
pray
About

JOURNAL &
NOTEBOOK

BARBOUR BOOKS
An Imprint of Barbour Publishing, Inc.

Published by Barbour Books, an imprint of Barbour Publishing, Inc., 1810 Barbour Drive, Uhrichsville, Ohio 44683, www.barbourbooks.com

Our mission is to inspire the world with the life-changing message of the Bible.

Member of the
Evangelical Christian
Publishers Association

INTRODUCTION

One day, Jesus told His disciples a story to show that they should always pray and never give up.

In Luke 18, Jesus told the parable of the persistent widow to teach His followers that they should never lose heart in bringing their requests before God. With Jesus as your mediator, you can approach the one true God—in total confidence—with your needs, concerns, desires, and praise. What an incredible privilege! What loving favor lavished on us! *We* can relentlessly pray to *Him*—the sovereign, Almighty Creator, the King of all kings!

So what kinds of things should you pray about? . . . First and foremost, worship and thank God for endless opportunities to come to Him in prayer. Then use these 501 prayer topics to help you develop deeper and dearer conversations with the One who loves you like no other—the One who sent His Son so you could have a relationship with Him and life that lasts forever.

1. To confess your sin
2. To receive salvation

....
....
....
....
....
....
....
....
....
....
....
....
....

Have you confessed your sin, acknowledged your need of a Savior, and accepted Jesus Christ? Praise and thank God for the gift of salvation through His Son!

3. To praise God for salvation

4. To thank God for salvation

My heart's desire and prayer to God for
them is that they may be saved.
ROMANS 10:1 ESV

5. For those who don't know Christ
6. For opportunities to share Christ with others

_Who specifically do you need to pray for today
that they will come to accept Jesus Christ?_

7. For salvation for family and friends

8. For salvation for coworkers and neighbors

This is good and pleases God our Savior, who wants everyone to be saved and to understand the truth.
1 TIMOTHY 2:3–4 NLT

9. For an increased desire to draw near to God

10. For help in making time to pray

How do you make time with God your top priority?

11. For help in making time to read God's Word
12. For help in memorizing God's Word

The LORD is near to all who call on him,
to all who call on him in truth.
PSALM 145:18 ESV

13. For wisdom to have the right priorities

14. For determination to keep the right priorities

*What things threaten to interfere with
the right priorities in your life?*

15. For wisdom to identify idols in your life

16. For help in ridding your life of idols

Jesus answered, "It is written:
'Worship the Lord your God and serve him only.'"
LUKE 4:8 NIV

17. For the ability to be still before God

18. For a mind and heart focused on God

....

....

....

....

....

....

....

....

....

....

....

....

....

....

....

....

How do you practice stillness before God?

19. To have eyes turned away from the world

20. To have eyes turned on Jesus

"Be still, and know that I am God; I will be exalted among the nations, I will be exalted in the earth."

PSALM 46:10 NIV

21. To grow in love

22. To grow in joy

What fruits of the Spirit are abundant in your life?

23. To grow in peace

24. To grow in patience

But the Holy Spirit produces this kind of fruit in our lives:
love, joy, peace, patience, kindness, goodness,
faithfulness, gentleness, and self-control.
GALATIANS 5:22–23 NLT

25. To grow in kindness and goodness
26. To grow in faithfulness

How will you keep cultivating the fruit of the Spirit in your life?

27. To grow in gentleness

28. To grow in self-control

There is no law against these things!
GALATIANS 5:23 NLT

29. For your own needs
30. For your friends' needs

_Do you ever feel overwhelmed by all your needs
and the needs of loved ones? Pray and imagine placing
them in your heavenly Father's loving hands._

31. For a child's needs

32. For a stranger's needs

*But my God shall supply all your need according
to his riches in glory by Christ Jesus.*
PHILIPPIANS 4:19 KJV

33. For your family's needs
34. For needs in your church family

How has God provided for your needs in the past?
Trust Him also to provide for the future.

35. For coworkers' needs

36. For neighbors' needs

The eyes of all look to you in hope; you give them their food as they need it. When you open your hand, you satisfy the hunger and thirst of every living thing.

PSALM 145:15–16 NLT

37. For your work to honor God
38. For good work relationships

How might you focus on making every aspect
of your job an act of praise to God?

39. For favor with those in authority at work

40. For advancement at work, according to God's will

Whatever you do, work heartily,
as for the Lord and not for men.
COLOSSIANS 3:23 ESV

41. For blessing in health
42. For blessing in relationships

God wants to give you the best kinds of blessings!
How has He blessed you in the past?
What blessings are you asking for in the future?

43. For blessing in finances

44. For blessing in the desires of your heart

"If you sinful people know how to give good gifts to your children, how much more will your heavenly Father give the Holy Spirit to those who ask him."

LUKE 11:13 NLT

45. For discipline to tithe regularly
46. For cheerfulness in giving

Are you faithful in giving back a portion of your finances
to God? If so, how has God blessed you because of it?

47. For wisdom in giving
48. For generosity in giving

Whoever sows sparingly will also reap sparingly, and whoever sows generously will also reap generously. Each of you should give what you have decided in your heart to give, not reluctantly or under compulsion, for God loves a cheerful giver.

2 CORINTHIANS 9:6–7 NIV

49. For the global church
50. For your home church

How do you see the church effectively building God's kingdom?
In what ways are you contributing?

51. For pastors and church leaders all over the world
52. For your local pastor and church leaders

Remember your leaders who taught you the word of God.
Think of all the good that has come from their lives,
and follow the example of their faith.
HEBREWS 13:7 NLT

53. To be active in ministry
54. To know and use your spiritual gifts

....
....
....
....
....
....
....
....
....
....
....
....
....
....
....
....

What special talents and gifts has God given you?
How might you use those to serve Him?

55. To help build God's kingdom
56. To promote unity in the church

They all joined together constantly in prayer, along with the women and Mary the mother of Jesus, and with his brothers.

ACTS 1:14 NIV

57. For world leaders

58. For national leaders

Are you pleased or disappointed with national and local leaders? What does God call you to do for them? How can you be a leader?

59. For community leaders
60. To be a leader of others

....

....

....

....

....

....

....

....

....

....

....

....

....

*First of all, then, I urge that supplications, prayers,
intercessions, and thanksgivings be made for all people,
for kings and all who are in high positions, that we may lead
a peaceful and quiet life, godly and dignified in every way.*
1 TIMOTHY 2:1–2 ESV

61. For help in practicing healthy eating habits

62. For help in getting regular exercise

....

....

....

....

....

....

....

....

....

....

....

....

....

....

....

....

....

....

....

....

Do you take good care of your body?
What goals do you have for improving your health?

63. For help in getting sufficient rest

64. For help in establishing good habits

Do you not know that your bodies are temples of the Holy Spirit, who is in you, whom you have received from God? You are not your own; you were bought at a price. Therefore honor God with your bodies.

1 CORINTHIANS 6:19–20 NIV

65. Praise God for being Elohim, the strong Creator God

66. Praise God for being Jehovah, your Lord and Master

*How has God shown you that He is Creator,
Lord, Master over all, the Most High God?*

67. Praise God for being Adonai, the Master over all

68. Praise God for being El Elyon, the Most High God

_For you, LORD, are the Most High over all the earth;
you are exalted far above all gods._
PSALM 97:9 NIV

69. To hear and obey God (not man)
70. To trust that God's commands are not burdens

How are God's commandments different
from the ways of the world?

71. To delight in keeping God's commands
72. To hold fast to God's commands

For this is the love of God, that we keep his commandments.
And his commandments are not burdensome.

1 JOHN 5:3 ESV

73. To love God with all your heart
74. To love God with all your soul

....

....

....

....

....

....

....

....

....

....

....

....

....

....

How do you show your love for God?
How can you continue to develop your love for Him?

75. To love God with all your strength

76. To love your neighbor as yourself

"Teacher, which is the greatest commandment in the Law?"
Jesus replied: " 'Love the Lord your God with all your heart
and with all your soul and with all your mind.' This is the first
and greatest commandment. And the second is
like it: 'Love your neighbor as yourself.' "
MATTHEW 22:36–39 NIV

77. For wisdom

78. For discernment

When have you most needed wisdom and discernment?
Why are wisdom and discernment so important?

79. For clarity
80. For a sober mind

....

....

....

....

....

....

....

....

....

....

....

....

....

....

....

If you need wisdom, ask our generous God, and he will give it to you. He will not rebuke you for asking.

JAMES 1:5 NLT

81. For strength
82. For boldness

In what areas of life do you feel the weakest and most timid?

83. For endurance

84. For a strong sense of God's power within

*For the Spirit God gave us does not make us timid,
but gives us power, love and self-discipline.*

2 TIMOTHY 1:7 NIV

85. For the ability to stand strong against temptation
86. For protection from the devil

....

....

....

....

....

....

....

....

....

....

....

....

....

....

....

....

....

....

....

....

....

....

....

When do you feel most attacked and tempted by the devil?

87. For deliverance from the evil one
88. For vigilance against the evil one

Your enemy the devil prowls around like a roaring lion looking for someone to devour. Resist him, standing firm in the faith.
1 PETER 5:8–9 NIV

89. For laughter

90. For joy, even in suffering

*What makes you laugh and smile the most? How can you
be aware of the joy God offers in all circumstances?*

91. For a desire to share joy with others

92. For delight in the smallest of blessings

Bring joy to your servant, Lord,
for I put my trust in you.
PSALM 86:4 NIV

93. Praise God for being your Dwelling Place
94. Praise God for being the Desired of All Nations

What does it mean that God is your constant dwelling place?
How does that idea comfort you?

95. Praise God for being Emmanuel

96. Praise God for being the Excellent One

Lord, you have been our dwelling place in all generations.
PSALM 90:1 ESV

97. For healing from sickness
98. For relief from pain

....
....
....
....
....
....
....
....
....
....
....
....
....
....
....
....
....
....
....
....
....
....

What illnesses and pain has God delivered you from?
Pray and trust Him for the future too.

99. For peace to prevail over anxiety issues

100. For comfort in grieving

....

....

....

....

....

....

....

....

....

....

....

....

....

If Christ is in you, then even though your body is subject to death because of sin, the Spirit gives life because of righteousness. And if the Spirit of him who raised Jesus from the dead is living in you, he who raised Christ from the dead will also give life to your mortal bodies because of his Spirit who lives in you.

ROMANS 8:10–11 NIV

101. To value time alone with God

102. For an overwhelming sense of God's presence when feeling lonely

....

....

....

....

....

....

....

....

....

....

....

....

....

....

....

Do you prefer to be alone or with other people? How can you model Jesus' example of balancing time with others with frequent time alone with God?

103. For good fellowship times with other Christians

104. For opportunities to reach out to those who feel lonely

May the grace of the Lord Jesus Christ, and the love of God,
and the fellowship of the Holy Spirit be with you all.
2 CORINTHIANS 13:14 NIV

105. For godly friendships
106. For deeper relationships with others

How do your friendships honor God?

107. For good mentors in your life
108. For people you can mentor

And let us consider how to stir up one another to love and good works, not neglecting to meet together, as is the habit of some, but encouraging one another, and all the more as you see the Day drawing near.

HEBREWS 10:24–25 ESV

109. For persecuted Christians to have hope and strength

110. For the persecutors of Christians to experience a true heart-change and to repent

....

....

....

....

....

....

....

....

....

....

....

....

....

....

....

*How must it feel to be brutally persecuted for faith in Jesus?
Commit to pray regularly for persecuted
Christians around the world.*

111. For the loved ones of persecuted Christians to have comfort and peace

112. For God to work good from the evil of persecution

"Blessed are those who are persecuted because of righteousness, for theirs is the kingdom of heaven."
MATTHEW 5:10 NIV

113. Praise God for being El Emunah, the faithful God
114. Praise God for being Elohei Tehillati, God of my praise

How has God shown you His great faithfulness?
How can you offer Him faithfulness in return?

115. Praise God for being El Hakabodh, the God of glory

116. Praise God for being Elohim Chayim, the living God

Honor the LORD for the glory of his name. Worship the LORD in the splendor of his holiness. The voice of the LORD echoes above the sea. The God of glory thunders. The LORD thunders over the mighty sea.

PSALM 29:2–3 NLT

117. For missionary work around the world
118. For safety and boldness for missionaries

What missionaries around the world do you know?
Make them a regular part of your prayer life.

119. To be a missionary wherever God places you

120. For all Christians to be missionaries and fulfill the Great Commission

"Go and make disciples of all nations, baptizing them in the name of the Father and of the Son and of the Holy Spirit, and teaching them to obey everything I have commanded you. And surely I am with you always, to the very end of the age."

MATTHEW 28:19–20 NIV

121. For a strong sense of God's purpose for you day by day
122. For good works to be done through you

What purposes has God laid on your heart for
His glory and to further His kingdom?

123. For help in letting go of things that don't produce good fruit in you

124. For connections and relationships that help you bear good fruit

....
....
....
....
....
....
....
....
....
....
....
....

"You didn't choose me. I chose you. I appointed you to go and produce lasting fruit, so that the Father will give you whatever you ask for, using my name."
JOHN 15:16 NLT

125. For increasing faith
126. For help in overcoming unbelief

What causes your faith to falter at times? What specific ways are you asking God to help you combat unbelief and have greater faith?

127. To see God's work in all things
128. To see God's glory in all of creation

Jesus asked the boy's father, "How long has he been like this?"
"From childhood," he answered. "It has often thrown him into
fire or water to kill him. But if you can do anything, take pity
on us and help us." " 'If you can'?" said Jesus. "Everything is
possible for one who believes." Immediately the boy's father
exclaimed, "I do believe; help me overcome my unbelief!"

MARK 9:21–24 NIV

129. For the ability to accept constructive criticism in your life

130. For the ability to lovingly speak hard things to others

Do you find it easy or hard to hear constructive criticism?
How can you learn and grow from it, and how can
you lovingly give it to others?

131. For more encouragers in your life

132. For opportunities to encourage others

Preach the word; be prepared in season and out of season;
correct, rebuke and encourage—with great
patience and careful instruction.

2 TIMOTHY 4:2 NIV

133. For honesty in all things
134. For the world to love God's truth

....

....

....

....

....

....

....

....

....

....

....

....

....

....

....

....

....

....

....

....

....

*Are there times or areas in your life where you
find it hard to be completely honest?*

135. For opportunities to promote truth
136. For liars to be revealed

The Lord detests lying lips, but he delights in those who tell the truth.

137. To be a peacemaker
138. To deal with conflict wisely

Do you avoid conflict or thrive on conflict?
Are you honoring God when it comes to conflict?

139. To know when to engage in and when to avoid conflict

140. To be full of mercy

Wherever there is jealousy and selfish ambition, there you will find disorder and evil of every kind. But the wisdom from above is first of all pure. It is also peace loving, gentle at all times, and willing to yield to others. It is full of mercy and the fruit of good deeds. It shows no favoritism and is always sincere. And those who are peacemakers will plant seeds of peace and reap a harvest of righteousness.

JAMES 3:16–18 NLT

141. For God's praise to be continually on your lips
142. To be careful in the words you speak

Do you feel like you have control over what you say?
If not, how might you choose your words more carefully?

143. To speak words of hope and life

144. To avoid foolish, damaging talk

*Do not let any unwholesome talk come out of your mouths,
but only what is helpful for building others up according
to their needs, that it may benefit those who listen.*

EPHESIANS 4:29 NIV

145. For daily bread

146. To trust that God provides one day at a time

What worries you about tomorrow? Focus your thoughts
and praise on what God has provided today,
and trust that He will do the same tomorrow.

147. To stop worrying overly much about finances

148. To store up treasure in heaven

"Look at the birds of the air; they do not sow or reap or store away in barns, and yet your heavenly Father feeds them. Are you not much more valuable than they? Can any one of you by worrying add a single hour to your life?"

MATTHEW 6:26–27 NIV

149. Praise God for being El Kanna, the jealous God

150. Praise God for being Elohei Ma'uzzi, God of my strength

What does it mean that God is a jealous God?

151. Praise God for being Elohim Kedoshim, the holy God

152. Praise God for being Elohim Machase Lanu, God our refuge

Trust in him at all times, you people; pour out your hearts to him, for God is our refuge.

153. For humility

154. For forgiveness from those you've sinned against

....

....

....

....

....

....

....

....

....

....

....

....

....

....

....

....

Are there current areas or relationships in your life where you need to humbly ask God and others for forgiveness? Will you commit to regularly examine this aspect of your life?

155. For forgiveness from God

156. For assurance that God removes sin from you

If we confess our sins, he is faithful and just to forgive us
our sins and to cleanse us from all unrighteousness.
1 JOHN 1:9 ESV

157. For the ability to forgive others

158. For a tender heart toward those who sin against you

Are you holding out on forgiving someone for wrong done against you? How can you keep a tender heart and be more forgiving in the future?

159. For grace to treat others better than they deserve

160. For increased gratitude that Christ treats you better than you deserve

Be kind to one another, tenderhearted,
forgiving one another, as God in Christ forgave you.
EPHESIANS 4:32 ESV

161. For power over sin and temptation

162. For wisdom to flee from dangerous and tempting situations

Describe ways you've fled from sin.
What lessons did you learn for the future?

163. For God's truth over your own fickle feelings
164. For God's truth over Satan's lies

Deliver me from my enemies, O LORD!
I have fled to you for refuge.
PSALM 143:9 ESV

165. To fully experience God's love for you

166. To have confidence that nothing can ever separate you from God's love

....

....

....

....

....

....

....

....

....

....

....

....

....

....

....

....

Do you ever fear that you are separated from God's love? Commit to fighting that lie.

167. To understand how wide and long and high and deep is God's love

168. To never stop being overwhelmed and thrilled by God's love

May you have the power to understand, as all God's people should, how wide, how long, how high, and how deep his love is. May you experience the love of Christ, though it is too great to understand fully. Then you will be made complete with all the fullness of life and power that comes from God.

EPHESIANS 3:18–19 NLT

169. To have more love for others
170. To have more compassion for others

....

....

....

....

....

....

....

....

....

....

....

....

....

....

....

....

....

....

In what ways do you actively demonstrate love and
compassion to others? How can you do this more and more?

171. To have more empathy for others

172. For more opportunities to meet others' needs

The end of the world is coming soon. Therefore, be earnest
and disciplined in your prayers. Most important of all,
continue to show deep love for each other,
for love covers a multitude of sins.

1 PETER 4:7–8 NLT

173. Praise God for being your Comforter
174. Praise God for being your Commander

_How do you feel knowing that God is both a loving
Comforter and a mighty Commander?_

175. Praise God for being the Cornerstone
176. Praise God for being your Deliverer

I love you, LORD, my strength. The LORD is my rock, my fortress and my deliverer; my God is my rock, in whom I take refuge, my shield and the horn of my salvation, my stronghold.

PSALM 18:1–2 NIV

177. For the Gospel to spread throughout the world
178. For more translators and deliverers of God's Word

How are you actively helping to spread the Gospel
of Jesus Christ? Praise God that you can contribute!

179. That God will open new doors of ministry

180. That God's people will recognize new open doors of ministry

"And this gospel of the kingdom will be proclaimed throughout the whole world as a testimony to all nations, and then the end will come."

MATTHEW 24:14 ESV

181. To trust that God cares about your anxiety
182. To cast all your anxiety on Him

....
....
....
....
....
....
....
....
....
....
....
....
....
....
....
....
....
....
....

Write down your anxious thoughts and give them
to God, because He cares about each one!

183. To stop worrying about what you can't control

184. To trust that nothing is impossible with God

---

*Do not be anxious about anything, but in every situation,
by prayer and petition, with thanksgiving, present your
requests to God. And the peace of God, which transcends
all understanding, will guard your hearts
and your minds in Christ Jesus.*

PHILIPPIANS 4:6–7 NIV

185. For food for those who are hungry

186. For provision for those who are poor

....
....
....
....
....
....
....
....
....
....
....
....
....
....
....
....
....

Have you ever been poor and hungry? How has God provided?
How can you help others who are poor and hungry?

187. For freedom for the enslaved

188. For rescue for the abused

For he will deliver the needy who cry out,
the afflicted who have no one to help.
PSALM 72:12 NIV

189. For healing for those who are sick
190. For courage for those who are afraid

Are you suffering from an illness? What about fear?
Write down your needs and trust God to help.

191. For power for the oppressed

192. For good work for those who are idle

"Learn to do good; seek justice, correct oppression;
bring justice to the fatherless, plead the widow's cause."

ISAIAH 1:17 ESV

193. To stand apart from the world
194. To be transformed with a renewed mind

Are there ways in which your life is too much like the world?
How can you actively renew your mind with
the goodness of God's ways?

195. To know God's will

196. To delight in God's good, pleasing, and perfect will

....

....

....

....

....

....

....

....

....

....

....

....

....

....

....

Do not conform to the pattern of this world, but be transformed by the renewing of your mind. Then you will be able to test and approve what God's will is—his good, pleasing and perfect will.

ROMANS 12:2 NIV

197. Praise God for being El Nekamoth, the God who avenges

198. Praise God for being Elohenu Olam, our everlasting God

Do you trust that God will avenge wrongdoing in the world?

199. Praise God for being Elohim Ozer Li, God my helper

200. Praise God for being El Roi, the God who sees me

_____

_____

_____

_____

_____

_____

_____

_____

_____

_____

_____

_____

_____

_____

_____

She gave this name to the LORD who spoke to her:
"You are the God who sees me," for she said,
"I have now seen the One who sees me."
GENESIS 16:13 NIV

201. To think about what is true
202. To think about what is honorable

Focus your thoughts and journaling today on what is true, honorable, right, and pure in your life.

203. To think about what is right
204. To think about what is pure

Finally, brothers and sisters, whatever is true,
whatever is noble, whatever is right,
whatever is pure. . .think about such things.
PHILIPPIANS 4:8 NIV

205. To think about what is lovely
206. To think about what is admirable

Focus your thoughts and journaling today on things that are lovely, admirable, excellent, and worthy of praise. Strive to do this every day.

207. To think about what is excellent

208. To think about what is worthy of praise

*Whatever is lovely, whatever is admirable—if anything is
excellent or praiseworthy—think about such things.*
PHILIPPIANS 4:8 NIV

209. To set healthy boundaries in relationships

210. To love and care for yourself in God-honoring ways

....

....

....

....

....

....

....

....

....

....

....

....

....

....

....

....

How can you care for others while also
remembering to take good care of yourself?

211. To be willing to confront sin in others in loving ways

212. To be willing to confess sin in your own
life in humble ways

_____

_____

_____

_____

_____

_____

_____

_____

_____

_____

_____

_____

"If another believer sins, rebuke that person; then if there is repentance, forgive. Even if that person wrongs you seven times a day and each time turns again and asks forgiveness, you must forgive."

LUKE 17:3–4 NLT

213. To be quick to listen
214. To be slow to speak

Do you love to talk, or would you rather quietly listen?
What are the benefits of both, and how can you balance them?

215. To be slow to become angry

216. To not just hear the Word but do the Word

My dear brothers and sisters, take note of this: Everyone should be quick to listen, slow to speak and slow to become angry.

JAMES 1:19 NIV

217. For your words to match your actions

218. To do good deeds without looking to receive praise

_Have you witnessed hypocrites in your life and
in the church? How do they make you feel?
How can you avoid being like them?_

219. To do good deeds in direct obedience to God

220. To take a close look at yourself before judging others

We know that we have come to know him if we keep his commands. Whoever says, "I know him," but does not do what he commands is a liar, and the truth is not in that person. But if anyone obeys his word, love for God is truly made complete in them. This is how we know we are in him: Whoever claims to live in him must live as Jesus did.

1 JOHN 2:3–6 NIV

221. To remember you will give an account of yourself to God
222. To realize the power of your words

One day you will give an account of yourself to God.
Write down scriptures that help remind you
to act accordingly to please God.

223. To keep a tight rein on your tongue
224. To have gracious speech

Nothing in all creation is hidden from God's sight.
Everything is uncovered and laid bare before the
eyes of him to whom we must give account.
HEBREWS 4:13 NIV

225. To respond gently

226. To remember that harsh words lead to anger

Is it a struggle for you to speak softly? Why or why not?

227. To keep a guard over your mouth

228. To have a door on your lips

....
....
....
....
....
....
....
....
....
....
....
....
....
....

Set a guard over my mouth, LORD;
keep watch over the door of my lips.
PSALM 141:3 NIV

229. To avoid getting caught up in outward beauty

230. To cultivate beauty that comes from within

*How can you focus less on outward appearance
and more on a person's heart?*

231. To know physical training has value,
but godliness has greater value

232. To know that charm is deceptive and beauty is fleeting,
but a healthy fear of the Lord is to be praised

"The LORD does not look at the things people look at.
People look at the outward appearance,
but the LORD looks at the heart."
1 SAMUEL 16:7 NIV

233. Praise God for being the Bright Morning Star
234. Praise God for being your Creator

....

....

....

....

....

....

....

....

....

....

....

....

....

How do you feel knowing that your Savior
is called the Bright Morning Star?

235. Praise God for being your Good Shepherd
236. Praise God for being the Chosen One

"I am the good shepherd. The good shepherd lays down his life for the sheep."

JOHN 10:11 NIV

237. To remember that the fear of God is the beginning of all knowledge

238. To increase in learning continually

In what ways can you actively continue to learn and increase your knowledge of God's truths?

239. To increase in wisdom and stature

240. To gain favor with God and others

And Jesus grew in wisdom and stature,
and in favor with God and man.
LUKE 2:52 NIV

241. To delight in children
242. To never hinder children

....
....
....
....
....
....
....
....
....
....
....
....
....
....

Who are the children in your life? How do they delight you?
Write down their names and pray specifically
for each one of them.

243. To care for children
244. To be more childlike in your faith

And they were bringing children to him that he might touch them, and the disciples rebuked them. But when Jesus saw it, he was indignant and said to them, "Let the children come to me; do not hinder them, for to such belongs the kingdom of God. Truly, I say to you, whoever does not receive the kingdom of God like a child shall not enter it." And he took them in his arms and blessed them, laying his hands on them.

MARK 10:13–16 ESV

245. To be wary of false prophets

246. To test what you hear against the truths of God's Word

....

....

....

....

....

....

....

....

....

....

....

....

....

....

....

....

....

....

....

....

....

....

Write down your experiences with hearing false prophets.
What lessons did you learn?

247. For your heart to be guarded against empty teachings of the world

248. To have roots that grow deep into Jesus for a strong spiritual foundation

Let your roots grow down into him, and let your lives be built on him. Then your faith will grow strong in the truth you were taught, and you will overflow with thankfulness. Don't let anyone capture you with empty philosophies and high-sounding nonsense that come from human thinking and from the spiritual powers of this world, rather than from Christ.

COLOSSIANS 2:7–8 NLT

249. Praise God for being El Sali, God my Rock
250. Praise God for being El Shaddai, God Almighty

*How do you feel knowing that God
is Almighty and He is your Rock?*

251. Praise God for being Elohim Tsebaoth, the God of hosts

252. Praise God for being El Simchath Gili, God my exceeding joy

Then I will go to the altar of God, to God my exceeding joy, and I will praise you with the lyre, O God, my God.

PSALM 43:4 ESV

253. For strength to do God's will
254. For guidance to be successful

How do you measure success in your life? What does the Bible
say about it? In what ways do you seek God's will?

255. To lean not on your own understanding

256. To remember that God's ways are higher than human ways

Trust in the LORD with all your heart and lean not on your own understanding; in all your ways submit to him, and he will make your paths straight.

PROVERBS 3:5–6 NIV

257. To rejoice in the gift of each day

258. To never take a brand-new day for granted

_____

_____

_____

_____

_____

_____

_____

_____

_____

_____

_____

_____

_____

_____

_____

As you end the day, not knowing if it will be your last,
how can you be sure you've lived it in a
way that is pleasing to God?

259. To trust that God numbers your days

260. To trust that your times are in His hands

But I trust in you, LORD; I say, "You are my God."
My times are in your hands.
PSALM 31:14–15 NIV

261. To be mindful of what you watch

262. To be discerning in your music choices

In what ways do you guard your mind against
the evil things of the world?

263. To be selective about what you read

264. To be careful who influences you

....

....

....

....

....

....

....

....

....

....

....

....

....

....

....

....

Do not love the world or the things in the world. If anyone loves the world, the love of the Father is not in him. For all that is in the world—the desires of the flesh and the desires of the eyes and pride of life—is not from the Father but is from the world. And the world is passing away along with its desires, but whoever does the will of God abides forever.

1 JOHN 2:15–17 ESV

265. To avoid the temptation to be lazy

266. For strength to work hard, always doing your best

Are you ever tempted to be lazy? What's the difference between getting good rest and being lazy?

267. To give God credit for your ability to work

268. To have a humble spirit

It is God who works in you to will and to act
in order to fulfill his good purpose.
PHILIPPIANS 2:13 NIV

269. To be selfless

270. To hold loosely to material things

Is it hard for you to let go of material possessions? Why or why not?

271. To thank God for every good gift

272. To never love money

*As for the rich in this present age, charge them not to be
haughty, nor to set their hopes on the uncertainty of riches,
but on God, who richly provides us with everything to enjoy.
They are to do good, to be rich in good works, to be generous
and ready to share, thus storing up treasure for themselves
as a good foundation for the future, so that they
may take hold of that which is truly life.*

1 TIMOTHY 6:17–19 ESV

273. To be good a steward
274. To steer clear of jealousy

What does the Bible say about handling money?
Do you find it difficult to follow God's Word
when it comes to your finances?

275. To be content with what you have
276. To store up real treasure in heaven

"Do not store up for yourselves treasures on earth, where
moths and vermin destroy, and where thieves break in
and steal. But store up for yourselves treasures in heaven,
where moths and vermin do not destroy, and where
thieves do not break in and steal. For where your
treasure is, there your heart will be also."

MATTHEW 6:19–21 NIV

277. To fight discouragement
278. To avoid giving in to weariness

What causes you to grow weary and why?

279. To never give up hope in God and His promises

280. To continue to declare what God has done in your life

Why, my soul, are you downcast? Why so disturbed within me?
Put your hope in God, for I will yet praise him,
my Savior and my God.
PSALM 43:5 NIV

281. To be ready to share the reason for your hope in Christ Jesus

282. To boast in God alone

What answer will you give when others ask about your hope in Jesus?

283. To always be respectful of others

284. To live a holy life among others

*Be careful to live properly among your unbelieving neighbors.
Then even if they accuse you of doing wrong, they will
see your honorable behavior, and they will give
honor to God when he judges the world.*
1 PETER 2:12 NLT

285. To make good plans, but trust the Lord
to determine your steps

286. To submit to God and let Him make your paths straight

When you're making plans, how can you submit them to God?

287. To know that if it is according to God's will, you can do anything

288. To trust that God has good plans for you

Look here, you who say, "Today or tomorrow we are going to a certain town and will stay there a year. We will do business there and make a profit." How do you know what your life will be like tomorrow? Your life is like the morning fog— it's here a little while, then it's gone. What you ought to say is, "If the Lord wants us to, we will live and do this or that."

JAMES 4:13–15 NLT

289. Praise God for being wonderful
290. Praise God for being your Counselor

Knowing God is your wonderful Counselor, in what ways can you both talk to and listen to Him better?

291. Praise God for being the mighty God

292. Praise God for being the everlasting Father

For to us a child is born, to us a son is given; and the government shall be upon his shoulder, and his name shall be called Wonderful Counselor, Mighty God, Everlasting Father, Prince of Peace.

ISAIAH 9:6 ESV

293. For a willingness to learn

294. For a mind open to the wisdom of those who are older and wiser

What does it mean to be teachable as an adult?

295. For friends who make you a better person

296. To be a good example for younger people

Listen to advice and accept instruction,
that you may gain wisdom in the future.
PROVERBS 19:20 ESV

297. To endure through fiery trials
298. To avoid being thrown off course by trials

....
....
....
....
....
....
....
....
....
....
....
....
....
....
....
....
....
....
....
....

What are some of the most difficult trials you've undergone?
How has God helped you through them?

299. To delight in trials because of the good they can produce

300. To grow closer to God through trials

Dear friends, don't be surprised at the fiery trials you are going through, as if something strange were happening to you. Instead, be very glad—for these trials make you partners with Christ in his suffering, so that you will have the wonderful joy of seeing his glory when it is revealed to all the world.

1 PETER 4:12–13 NLT

301. To practice good discipline in all areas of your life
302. To teach the children in your life good discipline

....

....

....

....

....

....

....

....

....

....

....

....

....

....

....

....

Discipline should not be confused with punishment.
Do you find it easy or hard to practice discipline in your life?

303. To be thankful for God's discipline
304. To train for godliness

*No discipline is enjoyable while it is happening—it's painful!
But afterward there will be a peaceful harvest of right
living for those who are trained in this way.*

HEBREWS 12:11 NLT

305. To love what really matters

306. To remember this world is temporary

How can you enjoy life without loving the world?

307. To remember that what is seen is temporary
308. To know that what is unseen is eternal

So we fix our eyes not on what is seen, but on what is unseen,
since what is seen is temporary, but what is unseen is eternal.
2 Corinthians 4:18 niv

309. To have confidence in your identity in Christ

310. To believe you are fearfully and wonderfully made

....

....

....

....

....

....

....

....

....

....

....

....

....

....

What things threaten to steal your confidence?
How might you combat them?

311. To rejoice in being a child of God

312. To continue to become more and more like Jesus

....

....

....

....

....

....

....

....

....

....

....

....

....

I praise you, for I am fearfully and wonderfully made.
Wonderful are your works; my soul knows it very well.
PSALM 139:14 ESV

313. To know that although this life is full of pain and sorrow, good will win

314. Praise Jesus for the promise that He has overcome the world

There is no escape from pain and sorrow in this world, but there is joy in Christ anyway. What are your current joys and your hopes for your future eternal life with Him?

315. To trust that God is preparing a place for you

316. To trust that Jesus will return soon

"Do not let your hearts be troubled. You believe in God; believe also in me. My Father's house has many rooms; if that were not so, would I have told you that I am going there to prepare a place for you? And if I go and prepare a place for you, I will come back and take you to be with me that you also may be where I am. You know the way to the place where I am going."

JOHN 14:1–4 NIV

317. Praise God for being Alpha and Omega, the beginning and the end

318. Praise God for being the Ancient of Days

How do you feel knowing that your Father God is the Alpha and Omega and the Ancient of Days?

319. Praise God for being the Anointed One

320. Praise God for being the God of peace

For God is not a God of disorder but of peace.
1 CORINTHIANS 14:33 NIV

321. To trust that those who wait for the Lord
will renew their strength

322. To remember that the Lord is good
to those who wait for Him

....
....
....
....
....
....
....
....
....
....
....
....
....
....
....
....

*List the ways God has been good to you
during times of waiting.*

323. To trust that God's timing is not yours

324. To know and be grateful that God does not want anyone to perish

With the Lord a day is like a thousand years, and a thousand years are like a day. The Lord is not slow in keeping his promise, as some understand slowness. Instead he is patient with you, not wanting anyone to perish, but everyone to come to repentance.

2 PETER 3:8–9 NIV

325. To throw off anything that slows you down
326. To get rid of sin that entangles

What are some sins that slow you down?
How will you throw them off and get rid of them?

327. To run the race God has set before you

328. To fix your eyes on Jesus and all that He endured to help you endure

Therefore, since we are surrounded by such a great cloud of witnesses, let us throw off everything that hinders and the sin that so easily entangles. And let us run with perseverance the race marked out for us.
HEBREWS 12:1 NIV

329. For unreached people

330. For the Gospel to reach the ends of the earth

List and pray over each continent of the world, that the Gospel would reach all people in all places.

331. For each issue in the news headlines

332. For God's justice to prevail

Then Peter began to speak: "I now realize how true it is that God does not show favoritism but accepts from every nation the one who fears him and does what is right."

ACTS 10:34–35 NIV

333. For all people to value the smallest of human lives as made in the image of God

334. For defense and care for the helpless and elderly

Praise God that you are made in His image! In what ways can you encourage others to value all human life?

335. For the care of orphans and widows

336. For more families to adopt orphans

Pure and genuine religion in the sight of God the Father means caring for orphans and widows in their distress and refusing to let the world corrupt you.

JAMES 1:27 NLT

337. For God to raise up the humble

338. For God's good commands to be honored throughout the world

....
....
....
....
....
....
....
....
....
....
....
....
....
....
....
....
....
....
....

How can you work to tear down pride and develop humility in your own life?

339. For God's name to be exalted throughout the world

340. For God's kingdom to expand throughout the world

Therefore God has highly exalted him and bestowed on him the name that is above every name, so that at the name of Jesus every knee should bow, in heaven and on earth and under the earth, and every tongue confess that Jesus Christ is Lord, to the glory of God the Father.
PHILIPPIANS 2:9–11 ESV

341. For the healing of unbelievers, that they would come to know God

342. For miraculous deliverances for those in need of rescue

List the miracles God has done in your life and the lives of others you know. Praise Him!

343. For God to establish strong Christians in government leadership

344. For the steadfast integrity of Christians in government leadership

....

....

....

....

....

....

....

....

....

....

....

....

....

....

First of all, then, I urge that supplications, prayers, intercessions, and thanksgivings be made for all people, for kings and all who are in high positions.
1 TIMOTHY 2:1–2 ESV

345. For the boldness of Christians in government leadership

346. For encouragement and stamina for Christians in government leadership

Why is it so easy to complain about government leaders, but so hard to remember to pray for them? List specific government leaders you commit to pray for regularly.

347. For safety in schools

348. For courage and protection for students, teachers, and staff

The angel of the LORD encamps around those
who fear him, and delivers them.
PSALM 34:7 ESV

349. For God to be proclaimed and exalted in schools

350. For Christian students and staff in schools to spread the love of Christ

What are some of your best and worst school memories?

351. For those who serve in the military, risking their lives to defend freedom

352. For Christians in the military to share the love of Christ

*Fear not, for I am with you; be not dismayed, for I am
your God; I will strengthen you, I will help you,
I will uphold you with my righteous right hand.*

ISAIAH 41:10 ESV

353. Thank God for all who have given their lives to defend freedom

354. Thank God for religious freedom

Imagine living in a place where you did not have the freedom to openly follow and worship Jesus Christ. How would your life be different? Pray for those for whom this experience is reality.

355. For continued religious freedom to proclaim the Gospel of Christ

356. For religious freedom to spread throughout the world

The LORD is near to all who call on him, to all who call on him in truth. He fulfills the desire of those who fear him; he also hears their cry and saves them.

PSALM 145:18–19 ESV

357. Praise God for being the Prince of Peace

358. Praise God for being Abba, your heavenly Daddy

How do you feel thinking of God Almighty
as your loving Daddy?

359. Praise God for being your Advocate

360. Praise God for being your All in All

My dear children, I write this to you so that you will not sin.
But if anybody does sin, we have an advocate with
the Father—Jesus Christ, the Righteous One.

1 JOHN 2:1 NIV

361. For marriages that honor God
362. For families that honor God

....

....

....

....

....

....

....

....

....

....

....

....

....

....

*List ways you can be more intentional about
honoring God in your relationships.*

363. For friendships that honor God

364. For households that serve the Lord

"But if you refuse to serve the LORD, then choose today whom you will serve. Would you prefer the gods your ancestors served beyond the Euphrates? Or will it be the gods of the Amorites in whose land you now live? But as for me and my family, we will serve the LORD."

JOSHUA 24:15 NLT

365. To be protected from evil spiritual forces by the full armor of God

366. To stand firm against evil

In what ways do God's truths help you stand firm against evil?

367. To have the belt of truth buckled around your waist

368. To have the breastplate of righteousness in place

For our struggle is not against flesh and blood, but against the rulers, against the authorities, against the powers of this dark world and against the spiritual forces of evil in the heavenly realms.

EPHESIANS 6:12 NIV

369. To have feet fitted with the readiness that comes from the Gospel

370. To take up the shield of faith to extinguish the flaming arrows of the evil one

....

....

....

....

....

....

....

....

....

....

....

....

....

....

How do you feel knowing that you are protected by the full armor of God?

371. To wear the helmet of salvation

372. To wield the sword of the Spirit, which is the Word of God

....

....

....

....

....

....

....

....

Therefore put on the full armor of God, so that when the day of evil comes, you may be able to stand your ground, and after you have done everything, to stand. Stand firm then, with the belt of truth buckled around your waist, with the breastplate of righteousness in place, and with your feet fitted with the readiness that comes from the gospel of peace. In addition to all this, take up the shield of faith, with which you can extinguish all the flaming arrows of the evil one. Take the helmet of salvation and the sword of the Spirit, which is the word of God.

EPHESIANS 6:13–17 NIV

373. Praise God for being Love

374. Praise God for being King of kings and Lord of lords

God is love. Write down and then thank God for
all the sources of His love in your life.

375. Praise God for being the Blessed and Holy Ruler

376. Praise God for being the Bread of Life

*Jesus replied, "I am the bread of life. Whoever comes to
me will never be hungry again. Whoever believes
in me will never be thirsty."*

JOHN 6:35 NLT

377. For a clean heart
378. For a renewed and steadfast spirit

Describe the feeling you have when you confess
your sin and let God clean out your heart.

379. For God to search your heart
380. For God to show you any offensive way in you

Search me, God, and know my heart; test me and know my anxious thoughts. See if there is any offensive way in me, and lead me in the way everlasting.
PSALM 139:23–24 NIV

381. To trust that worldly troubles are momentary

382. To trust that current troubles are achieving eternal glory

....

....

....

....

....

....

....

....

....

....

....

....

....

....

....

....

List your current troubles, and beside each one add the label is momentary *or* is achieving eternal glory.

383. Acknowledge that outwardly, you are wasting away

384. Praise God that inwardly, you are renewed day by day

*Therefore we do not lose heart. Though outwardly we are
wasting away, yet inwardly we are being renewed day by day.
For our light and momentary troubles are achieving for
us an eternal glory that far outweighs them all.*

2 Corinthians 4:16–17 NIV

385. Praise God for being your Shield
386. Praise God for being your Strong Tower

_Describe the ways you depend on God as
your Shield and Strong Tower._

387. Praise God for being your Teacher
388. Praise God for being the Vine

---

*"I am the vine; you are the branches. If you remain
in me and I in you, you will bear much fruit;
apart from me you can do nothing."*

JOHN 15:5 NIV

389. To trust that when you are hard-pressed on every side, you will not be crushed

390. To trust that when you are perplexed, you will not be in despair

....

....

....

....

....

....

....

....

....

....

List the ways you feel hard-pressed.
Beside each one, write, But I am not crushed.
List the ways you feel perplexed.
Beside each one, write, But I am not in despair.
List the ways you feel persecuted.
Beside each one, write, But I am not abandoned.
List the ways you feel knocked down.
Beside each one, write, But I am not destroyed.

391. To trust that when you are persecuted,
you will not be abandoned

392. To trust that when you are knocked down,
you will not be destroyed

We are hard pressed on every side, but not crushed; perplexed,
but not in despair; persecuted, but not abandoned;
struck down, but not destroyed. We always carry around
in our body the death of Jesus, so that the life of
Jesus may also be revealed in our body.

2 CORINTHIANS 4:8–10 NIV

393. For God's light to shine in the darkness
394. To walk in the light

_As a Christian, describe how your light affects
the darkness of the world around you._

395. To shine God's light before others

396. To proclaim God's excellence

"In the same way, let your light shine before others, that they may see your good deeds and glorify your Father in heaven."
MATTHEW 5:16 NIV

397. To be an imitator of God

398. To give yourself for others, as Christ gave Himself for you

....

....

....

....

....

....

....

....

....

....

....

....

Are you ever tempted to imitate others instead of God?
Describe how you can avoid this temptation.

399. To walk in love

400. To be a fragrant offering and sacrifice to God

Therefore be imitators of God, as beloved children.
And walk in love, as Christ loved us and gave himself
up for us, a fragrant offering and sacrifice to God.
EPHESIANS 5:1–2 ESV

401. To meditate on God's Word

402. To let God's Word be a lamp to your feet and a light to your path

....
....
....
....
....
....
....
....
....
....
....
....
....
....
....
....
....

Describe the difference between letting God's Word light your path and walking without God's Word.

403. To trust that all scripture is God-breathed

404. To store up God's Word in your heart to keep you from sin

All Scripture is God-breathed and is useful for teaching, rebuking, correcting and training in righteousness, so that the servant of God may be thoroughly equipped for every good work.

2 TIMOTHY 3:16–17 NIV

405. Praise God for being the Father
406. Praise God for being the Son

_Focus on God as three in one—Father, Son,
and Holy Spirit. What questions will you want
to ask in heaven about the Trinity?_

407. Praise God for being the Holy Spirit

408. Praise God for being faithful and true

The grace of the Lord Jesus Christ and the love of God and the fellowship of the Holy Spirit be with you all.

2 CORINTHIANS 13:14 ESV

409. To be lifted out of dark, slimy pits
410. To be set upon a rock

*Describe a time when you felt like you were stuck
in a slimy pit and God lifted you out.*

411. For firm places to stand

412. For new songs—new hymns of praise to God

He lifted me out of the slimy pit, out of the mud and mire;
he set my feet on a rock and gave me a firm place to stand.

PSALM 40:2 NIV

413. For an ever-increasing love for your enemies

414. For the desire to pray for those who persecute you

Only with God's love is it possible to love and pray for enemies and persecutors. Write down specific, fervent prayers asking Him to help you with this.

415. To seek God's kingdom
416. To seek God's righteousness

"But seek first the kingdom of God and his righteousness."
MATTHEW 6:33 ESV

417. That you would pray in secret for your Father to hear

418. That you would give in secret for your Father to see

*How can you be sure your prayers
and giving are for God's glory alone?*

419. That you would acknowledge that each day has enough trouble of its own

420. That you would not worry about tomorrow

"Therefore do not worry about tomorrow, for tomorrow will worry about itself. Each day has enough trouble of its own."

MATTHEW 6:34 NIV

421. Praise God for being your Fortress

422. Praise God for being your Foundation

Describe how God is a fortress and foundation to you.

423. Praise God for being your Fountain of Living Water
424. Praise God for being your Friend

"No longer do I call you servants, for the servant does not know what his master is doing; but I have called you friends, for all that I have heard from my Father I have made known to you."
JOHN 15:15 ESV

425. To abide in God
426. To let God's Word abide in you

To abide means to stay stable or to continue in something.
Describe how you might remain stable and
continue in God and His Word.

427. For accountability with others

428. For help in gently restoring others who are stuck in sin

Brothers and sisters, if someone is caught in a sin, you who live by the Spirit should restore that person gently. But watch yourselves, or you also may be tempted.
Galatians 6:1 niv

429. Praise God for being the Great High Priest

430. Praise God for being your Guide

If you don't let God guide you, where will you end up?

431. Praise God for being the Head of the Church

432. Praise God for being the Heir of All Things

But in these last days he has spoken to us by his
Son, whom he appointed the heir of all things,
through whom also he created the world.
HEBREWS 1:2 ESV

433. That you would give thanks in all circumstances

434. That you would make joyful noises to the Lord

What are your favorite ways to give thanks and make joyful noises to the Lord? List some of your favorite worship songs.

435. That you would serve God with gladness

436. That God's deeds would be known among all people

Serve the LORD with gladness:
come before his presence with singing.
PSALM 100:2 KJV

437. For a constant awareness of God's blessings
438. Praise God for being gracious

....

....

....

....

....

....

....

....

....

....

....

....

....

....

Write down as many of God's blessings as you can think of!

439. Praise God for being compassionate

440. Praise God for being slow to anger and abounding in love

Praise the LORD, my soul, and forget not all his benefits.
PSALM 103:2 NIV

441. Praise God for being your Hiding Place

442. Praise God for being your Hope

....

....

....

....

....

....

....

....

....

....

....

....

....

What stresses in life make you feel like you need God
as your Hiding Place? How do you feel knowing that
you can always run to Him for comfort and safety?

443. Praise God for being your Judge

444. Praise God for being the Light of the World

....

....

....

....

....

....

....

....

....

....

....

....

....

....

....

....

For the LORD is our judge; the LORD is our lawgiver;
the LORD is our king; he will save us.
ISAIAH 33:22 ESV

445. Praise God for being the Lion of the Tribe of Judah

446. Praise God for being the Living Water

Describe the refreshing, satisfying feeling
of knowing God as your Living Water.

447. Praise God for being merciful

448. Praise God for being Messiah

....
....
....
....
....
....
....
....
....
....
....
....
....

*But God, being rich in mercy, because of the great love
with which he loved us, even when we were dead in
our trespasses, made us alive together with
Christ—by grace you have been saved.*
EPHESIANS 2:4–5 ESV

449. To do everything without grumbling
450. To maintain a positive attitude

....

....

....

....

....

....

....

....

....

....

....

....

....

Avoiding all complaining and grumbling seems impossible!
How can you strive for this goal in your attitudes,
actions, and words?

451. To do nothing out of selfish ambition

452. To do nothing out of vain conceit

....

....

....

....

....

....

....

....

....

....

....

....

....

....

....

Do nothing out of selfish ambition or vain conceit. Rather, in humility value others above yourselves, not looking to your own interests but each of you to the interests of the others.

PHILIPPIANS 2:3–4 NIV

453. For wisdom when making big decisions

454. For peace when making difficult decisions

Do you make decisions easily or anxiously?

455. For the ability to deal well with change

456. Praise God for being unchanging

Jesus Christ is the same yesterday and today and forever.
HEBREWS 13:8 ESV

457. For an end to all prejudice and racism

458. For love for all people

What are some ways you can lovingly help end racism?

459. For God's people to be known for their love for one another

460. For God's people to love like Jesus loves

After this I looked, and behold, a great multitude that no one could number, from every nation, from all tribes and peoples and languages, standing before the throne and before the Lamb, clothed in white robes, with palm branches in their hands.

REVELATION 7:9 ESV

461. For protection from sexual immorality

462. For all people to appreciate God's design for sexuality

*With God's help, what boundaries can you put in place
to protect yourself from sexual immorality?*

463. For an end to human trafficking

464. For healing of sexual brokenness

Let marriage be held in honor among all, and let the
marriage bed be undefiled, for God will judge the
sexually immoral and adulterous.
HEBREWS 13:4 ESV

465. Praise God for being self-sufficient

466. Praise God for being able to do immeasurably more than you can ask or imagine

....

....

....

....

....

....

....

....

....

....

....

....

....

....

....

Describe how your prayer life changes when you focus on God's ability to do so much more than you could ask.

467. Praise God for being infinite

468. Praise God for being sovereign over all

Before the mountains were born or you brought forth the whole world, from everlasting to everlasting you are God.

PSALM 90:2 NIV

469. For doctors, nurses, and medical professionals

470. For advancements in medicine to fight disease

Praise God and pray for all the medical professionals in the world. How do you think medicine might improve if even more medical professionals knew Christ?

471. For more scientists and medical professionals to acknowledge God as Creator and Jesus as Savior

472. For specific people in your life currently fighting illness and disease

Is anyone among you sick? Let him call for the elders of the church, and let them pray over him, anointing him with oil in the name of the Lord.

JAMES 5:14 ESV

473. Praise God for being omnipotent, all-powerful

474. Praise God for being omniscient, all-knowing

God knows your every thought and deed, and those of every person on earth. How does that truth affect you and your walk with God?

475. Praise God for being omnipresent, always everywhere

476. Praise God for being holy

"Am I a God who is only close at hand?" says the LORD. "No, I am far away at the same time. Can anyone hide from me in a secret place? Am I not everywhere in all the heavens and earth?" says the LORD.

JEREMIAH 23:23–24 NLT

477. To know that real love is patient

478. To know that real love is kind

....
....
....
....
....
....
....
....
....
....
....
....
....
....
....
....
....

List ways you can strive to love others better.

479. To know that real love does not envy

480. To know that real love does not boast

....

....

....

....

....

....

....

....

....

....

....

....

....

*Love is patient and kind; love does not envy
or boast; it is not arrogant or rude.*

1 CORINTHIANS 13:4–5 ESV

481. To know that real love is not arrogant

482. To know that real love is not rude

....
....
....
....
....
....
....
....
....
....
....
....
....
....
....
....
....
....

What makes you act arrogantly or rudely sometimes?
Describe how you can rid yourself of arrogance and rudeness.

483. To know that real love does not insist on its own way

484. To know that real love is not irritable

[Love] does not insist on its own way;
it is not irritable or resentful.

1 CORINTHIANS 13:5 ESV

485. To know that real love is not resentful

486. To know that real love does not rejoice in wrongdoing

....

....

....

....

....

....

....

....

....

....

....

....

....

....

Are you holding on to any resentment?
Describe it here, and then let God take it away.

487. To know that real love rejoices with the truth

488. To know that real love never ends

[Love] does not rejoice at wrongdoing,
but rejoices with the truth.
1 CORINTHIANS 13:6 ESV

489. To be eager for prayer

490. To learn to pray like Jesus taught

*Write down and memorize the Lord's
Prayer found in Matthew 6.*

491. For God's name to be kept holy

492. For God's kingdom to come

"This, then, is how you should pray: 'Our Father in heaven, hallowed be your name, your kingdom come, your will be done, on earth as it is in heaven.'"

MATTHEW 6:9–10 NIV

493. For God's will to be done on earth as it is in heaven
494. For your daily needs to be met

List your most basic daily needs and then thank God that He always provides them.

495. For forgiveness of sins

496. For strength to offer forgiveness to those who sin against you

"Give us today our daily bread. And forgive us our debts, as we also have forgiven our debtors. And lead us not into temptation, but deliver us from the evil one."

MATTHEW 6:11–13 NIV

497. For protection from temptation and deliverance from evil

498. For all believers to pray for all things, all the time

....

....

....

....

....

....

....

....

....

....

....

....

....

....

....

What are your prayer goals? Create a schedule
for yourself and commit to it!

499. For discipline to engage in regular times of prayer

500. For assurance that the Holy Spirit intercedes when you don't know what to pray

In the same way, the Spirit helps us in our weakness. We do not know what we ought to pray for, but the Spirit himself intercedes for us through wordless groans. And he who searches our hearts knows the mind of the Spirit, because the Spirit intercedes for God's people in accordance with the will of God.

ROMANS 8:26–27 NIV

501. For Jesus to return quickly

Do you long for Christ's return? Write a love letter to Him, telling Him how much you long for His return and why!

....
....
....
....
....
....
....
....
....
....
....
....
....
....
....
....
....